Fun in Fall

T0014205

A FALL FESTIVAL

By Cliff Griswold

 Gareth Stevens
PUBLISHING

Please visit our website, www.garethstevens.com. For a free color catalog of all our high-quality books, call toll free 1-800-542-2595 or fax 1-877-542-2596.

Library of Congress Cataloging-in-Publication Data

Griswold, Cliff.
A fall festival / by Cliff Griswold.
p. cm. — (Fun in fall)
Includes index.
ISBN 978-1-4824-1769-2 (pbk.)
ISBN 978-1-4824-1770-8 (6-pack)
ISBN 978-1-4824-1768-5 (library binding)
1. Harvest festivals — Juvenile literature. 2. Autumn — Juvenile literature. I. Title.
GT4380.G75 2015
394.2—d23

First Edition

Published in 2015 by
Gareth Stevens Publishing
111 East 14th Street, Suite 349
New York, NY 10003

Editor: Ryan Nagelhout
Designer: Nicholas Domiano

Photo credits: Cover, p.1 (girl) wavebreakmedia/Shutterstock.com; cover, p.1 (background) © iStockphoto.com/ Propjockey; p. 5 Friedrich Schmidt/Photographer's Choice/Getty Images; pp. 7, 24 (band) Barry Blackburn/ Shutterstock.com; p. 9 Compassionate Eye Foundation/Digital Vision/Getty Images; p. 11 Karl R. Martin/ Shutterstock.com; pp. 13, 24 (candy apple) Sally Anscombe/Moment/Getty Images; p. 15 Osokina Liudmila/ Shutterstock.com; p. 17 Aleksei Potov/Shutterstock.com; p. 19 Zia Soleil/The Image Bank/Getty Images; p. 21 Alita Bobrov/Shutterstock.com; pp. 23, 24 (maze) Rich Koele/Shutterstock.com.

CPSIA compliance information: Batch #CW15GS: For further information contact Gareth Stevens, New York, New York at 1-800-542-2595.

Contents

My town has a party
in fall. It's a fall festival!

5

There is a live band!

7

People dance
to the music.

There is a lot
of good food.

I eat a candy apple!

My friend John gets some popcorn.

They have a farmers market, too.

17

My mom buys some pumpkins.

They even have
a corn maze.

CORN MAZE

My sister got lost inside!

23

Words to Know

band

candy apple

corn maze

Index

band 6

corn maze 20

farmers market 16

food 10

24